Toward the Winter Solstice

Also by Timothy Steele

Uncertainties and Rest

Sapphics against Anger and Other Poems

Missing Measures: Modern Poetry and the Revolt against Meter

The Color Wheel

Sapphics and Uncertainties: Poems 1970–1986

The Poems of J. V. Cunningham (editor)

All the Fun's in How You Say a Thing: An Explanation of Meter and Versification

Toward the Winter Solstice

New Poems

Timothy Steele

Swallow Press / Ohio University Press / *Athens, Ohio*

Swallow Press / Ohio University Press, Athens, Ohio 45701
www.ohio.edu/oupress

Printed in the United States of America

Swallow Press / Ohio University Press books are printed on acid-free paper ⊗ ™

14 13 12 11 10 09 08 07 06   5 4 3 2 1

Acknowledgments
Poems in this collection appeared originally in the following publications: *Bayou;*
Cadenza (England); *The Epigrammatist; Iambs and Trochees; Kenyon Review; Measure; The New*
Compass; The New Criterion; Order in Variety: Essays and Poems in Honor of Donald E. Stanford;
The Philadelphia Inquirer; Poetry ("Faustina," "The Middle Years," and "Toward the
Winter Solstice"); *Profile, Full Face; Smartish Pace; Southwest Review; The Threepenny Review;*
and *ZYZZYVA*. Ten poems were published subsequently in *Starr Farm Beach*, a limited-
edition chapbook from the Aralia Press. "For Victoria, Traveling in Europe" first
appeared as a broadside (illustrated by Abraham Brewster and printed by Ronald
Gordon at the Oliphant Press) that was commissioned by the Friends of the
Amherst College Library to mark the occasion of a reading the author gave to that
organization in October 1996.

Library of Congress Cataloging-in-Publication Data
Steele, Timothy.
   Toward the winter solstice : new poems / Timothy Steele.
      p. cm.
   ISBN-13: 978-0-8040-1090-0 (acid-free paper)
   ISBN-10: 0-8040-1090-0 (acid-free paper)
   ISBN-13: 978-0-8040-1091-7 (pbk. : acid-free paper)
   ISBN-10: 0-8040-1091-9 (pbk. : acid-free paper)
   I. Title.

PS3569.T33845T69 2006
811'.54—dc22

2005033881

in memory of Erland Gjessing

Contents

I

II

Daybreak, Benedict Canyon

Thick fog has filled the canyon overnight
And turned it to a sea of milky gray:
The steep-sloped chaparral and streets below
Are drowned from view; hilltops across the way
Form a low-lying archipelago
Upon the fog's smothering gulfs and shoals.
The scene, in the uncertain predawn light,
Recalls those Chinese landscapes on silk scrolls

In which mists haunt ravines, and clouds surround
Remote peaks fading to remoter skies.
The scene suggests, too, the apocalypse
The earth may suffer if sea levels rise.
This very deck could be a ghostly ship's
And I a lone survivor, cast by fate
Out on a flood as lifeless and profound
As the one Noah had to navigate.

Yet soon this world's specifics will revive
And banish fanciful analogies.
Some mourning doves, on airily whistling wings,
Will light in canyon-overhanging trees;
Damp breeze will test the tensile strength of strings,
Jeweled and soaking, that a spider's spun;
Cars snaking up along Mulholland Drive
Will flash their windshields at the rising sun.

The fog will drain; the canyon will evince
Toyon, buckthorn, and yucca, and restore
The ceanothus thickets that hide deer;
Houses will surface on the canyon floor.
The only ocean will be south of here
And glimpsed through a green hollow in a ridge,
Pacific in its sunny sparks and glints
Beyond San Pedro's Vincent Thomas Bridge.

Joanna, Wading

Too frail to swim, she nonetheless
Gingerly lifts her cotton dress
Clear of the lake, so she can wade
Where the descending sun has laid
A net of rippling, molten bands
Across the underwater sands.

Her toes dig, curling, in the cool
And fine-grained bottom; minnows school
Before her, tautly unified
In their suspended flash-and-glide;
Blue-brilliantly, a dragonfly
Encounters and skims round her thigh.

Despite age, all this still occurs.
The sun's companionably hers,
Its warmth suffusing blood and flesh,
While its light casts the mobile mesh
Whose glowing cords she swam among
In summertime when she was young.

Freudian Analysis

A luxury sedan sways round the curve,
Scattering rollerblading hockey players.
The motorist wears sunglasses, though night
Is gathering; his Great Dane, riding shotgun,
Leans from the window and barks furiously
At a bewildered terrier on the sidewalk.
Libidinous inanity! *Woof! Woof!*
I've got a Lexus and you've got a leash!
Driver and dog, quite clearly, haven't learned
That anybody can achieve an ego:
The real trick is resolving to transcend it.
Innocent ids, the boys regroup; one cuts
A circle sharply, swings his stick, and rifles
The plastic ball that serves as puck between
The pair of soda cans that serve as goalposts.
The superego's representatives,
Six ravens mob the disappearing car
Before they peel off, cawing, to the trees
While the small terrier—hair in his eyes,
His toenails clicking pavement—trots away,
Leading his owner homeward from their ramble.

Fountain in the City

The water climbed to a white crest, and fell,
Plashy and heavy, to a metal shell
Forever in a state of overflow
And then went dripping to the pool below.

The square had, otherwise, a leafless tree
And litter's swirling, sad agility;
And densely packed surrounding buildings made
The place, save at mid-day, a cheerless shade.

The homeless slumped on benches. Some would range
To pay phones and to news racks, hoping change
Lay in the coin-return cups; plump and gray,
Wing-clapping pigeons moved out of their way.

To pass the square at evening was to feel
The tension and the weight of stone and steel.
Striking a building's many-windowed face,
The sunset would glare redly back through space.

Yet still the cast-up flow would splash and spill,
As if with a magnanimous good will
Which all of the surrounding world had lost
But which no deprivation could exhaust.

In the Italian Alps

1913

Thick-carpeted and oaken warmth pervades
The evening common room of the hotel.
Lamps shed a modest light from tasseled shades;
Logs in the fireplace pop; somewhere a bell,
Announcing guests or a delivery, rings;
A couple on the couch let small talk lapse
And silently touch hands; an old gent snaps
His paper open and folds back its wings.

Our hero, at a window, has no use
For the postprandial comforts of the place:
The glass pane and the outer dark produce
A query-plagued reflection of his face.
Were she and he too volatile a mix?
Was his proposal the wrong note to strike?
Thoughts jolt each other till his brain feels like
The neighboring room where billiard balls trade clicks.

Reproaches would seem puerile, and embarrass
Them both; but he recalls the day they met—
How on that cobbled and grass-grown church terrace,
He sketched her, posed before the parapet,
Her arms outstretched upon its lichened shelf,
Her forehead shaded by her leghorn hat.
Perhaps if he reminded her of that
She'd pity him and would explain herself.

Perhaps . . . he chafes at this contingent mood
That, balking action, also serves to mar
His chances for productive solitude.
The old gent smokes and crushes a cigar,
Then heads for bed. The couple, too, retire—
The woman gathering the diaphanous flow
Of a long scarf about her as they go.
The young man turns for counsel to the fire,

Whose crackling flames still nimbly dart and branch
Against the chimney's throat. If, in a year,
Europe will smother in an avalanche
Deadlier than any triggered from up here,
If he himself will perish in a wood
Along the Marne, the truth remains that he
Burns now with all his puzzled ardency
To understand and to be understood.

And so he sits and writes her, and redoubles
His concentration as the hours pass;
The fire lets fall its glowing coals; small bubbles
Cling to the inside of a water glass;
Outside, a dark wind strengthens, scouring peaks
And lifting snowy veils from spur and crest,
Like a tormented soul refusing rest
Until it has discovered what it seeks.

In the Memphis Airport

Above the concourse, from a beam,
A little warbler pours forth song.
Beneath him, hurried humans stream:
Some draw wheeled suitcases along
Or from a beeping belt or purse
Apply a cell phone to an ear;
Some pause at banks of monitors
Where times and gates for flights appear.

Although by nature flight-endowed,
He seems too gentle to reproach
These souls who soon will climb through cloud
In first class, business class, and coach.
He may feel that it's his mistake
He's here, but someone ought to bring
A net to catch and help him make
His own connections north to spring.

He cheeps and trills on, swift and sweet,
Though no one outside hears his strains.
There, telescopic tunnels greet
The cheeks of their arriving planes;
A ground crew welcomes and assists
Luggage that skycaps, treating bags
Like careful ornithologists,
Banded with destination tags.

Jardin des Tuileries

The boy stood weeping in dismay,
Duffle-coated against the cold,
Watching his sailboat bob away
On a pool vast and granite-bowled.

No aid was asked, but seeing him,
I rolled my trousers to my knees
And waded from the basin's rim
To where the boat had sought the breeze

And, like a giant, lifted her
Up by the mast and centerboard.
Still sniffling, with "Merci, monsieur,"
The boy walked off, his loss restored.

This happened thirty years ago.
The trees were pollarded and bare,
The benches empty, and light snow
Fell to the flowerless parterre.

For several weeks, I'd launched campaigns
To all the tourist sites I could.
Most I've forgotten. What remains
Is how the boy drew up his hood,

Cradling his boat in winter light,
While I sat down and bowed to muse
Upon the gravel and draw tight
And tie the laces of my shoes.

Siglo de Oro

We draw distinctions between life and art,
But barriers break down. To our surprise,
Sancho and Don Quixote analyze
The very book in which they're taking part—
Pointing out places where the plot's not clear,
Disparaging the way their author's shaped
Their characters, until we feel that we're
Entranced within a story they've escaped.

Likewise, in *Las Meniñas,* self-portrayed,
Velázquez looks out at us as we stand
Before the work to which he's turned his hand.
Behind the princess and a kneeling maid,
He manages perspective, disinclined
To treat us as exterior to the scene,
So that we, in the background's mirror, find
Ourselves reflected as the King and Queen.

The painting's surface is itself profound,
And, by the artist's leave, we might presume
To pass into the picture and the room.
Indeed, already the Infanta, crowned
With light gold hair, invites us with her gaze;
Her female dwarf and second maid appear
To recognize us, while a man surveys
Proceedings from a doorway in the rear.

Illusion meets with similar success
When, at the puppet show, the Don lays waste
To villains made of paper pulp and paste
To save a puppet damsel in distress.
Drama absorbs him, and if now and then
He's crazily empathic and naïve,
He shows that life is most compelling when
It's shaped into persuasive make-believe.

Once, in the Prado's great Velázquez room,
We found a young art student copying
The Maids of Honor and examining
The old enigma of who spectates whom.
As if engaged in visual tit for tat,
He took the Master's pose and point of view,
While we who watched comprised a group like that
Formed by the princess and her retinue.

Another student, in a world of snow
And winter twilight, reads on to the end
Of *Don Quixote*; a few flakes descend
Irresolutely to the yard below.
And when the dying Don's illusions fail,
She weeps and sets the book back on its shelf
And then, in a ruled notebook, starts a tale
Or poem more substantial than herself.

April 27, 1937

General Ludendorff, two years before,
Had pushed the concept in his *Total War,*
And so it seemed a perfect time to see
If one could undermine an enemy
By striking its civilian population.
This proved a most effective innovation,
As the defenseless ancient Basque town learned:
Three-quarters of its buildings bombed and burned,
Its children and young wives were blown to bits
Or gunned down, when they fled, by Messerschmitts.
Shocked condemnations poured forth from the press,
But Franco triumphed; and, buoyed by success,
The Luftwaffe would similarly slam
Warsaw and Coventry and Rotterdam.

Berlin cheered these developments; but two
Can play such games—and usually do—
No matter how repellent or how bloody.
And Churchill was, as always, a quick study
And would adopt the tactic as his own,
Sending the RAF to blitz Cologne.
Devising better ways to carpet-bomb
(Which later were employed in Vietnam),
The Allies, in a show of aerial might,
Incinerated Dresden in a night
That left the good and evil to their fates,
While back in the untorched United States

Others approved an even darker plan
To coax a prompt surrender from Japan.

That day in Spain has taught us, to our cost,
That there are lines that never should be crossed;
The ignorance of leaders is not bliss
If they're intent on tempting Nemesis.
Each day we rise, and each day life goes on:
An author signs beneath a colophon;
Trucks carry freight through waves of desert heat;
A bat cracks, a crowd rises to its feet;
Huge jets lift to the sky, and, higher yet,
Float satellites that serve the Internet.
But still, despite our cleverness and love,
Regardless of the past, regardless of
The future on which all our hopes are pinned,
We'll reap the whirlwind, who have sown the wind.

Herb Garden

"And these, small, unobserved . . ."

JANET LEWIS

The lizard, an exemplar of the small,
Spreads fine, adhesive digits to perform
Vertical push-ups on a sunny wall;
Bees grapple spikes of lavender, or swarm
The dill's gold umbels or low clumps of thyme.
Bored with its trellis, a resourceful rose
Has found a nearby cedar tree to climb
And to festoon with floral furbelows.

Though the great, heat-stunned sunflower looks half dead
The way it, shepherd's crook–like, hangs its head,
The herbs maintain their modest self-command:
Their fragrances and colors warmly mix
While, quarrying between the pathway's bricks,
Ants build minute volcanoes out of sand.

The Swing

She shrieks as she sweeps past the earth
And, rising, pumps for all she's worth;
The chains she grips almost go slack;
Then, seated skyward, she drops back.

When swept high to the rear, she sees
Below the park the harbor's quays,
Cranes, rail tracks, transit sheds, and ranks
Of broad, round, silver storage tanks.

Her father lacks such speed and sight,
Though, with a push, he launched her flight.
Now, hands in pockets, he stands by
And, for her safety, casts his eye

Over the ground, examining
The hollow underneath the swing
Where, done with aerial assault,
She'll scuff, in passing, to a halt.

Anima

The way the latch clicks on the heart-shaped locket,
Assures us that our treasure's safe with it;
Leather creaks warmly when, to form a pocket,
We wrap a baseball in the catcher's mitt;
The yo-yo, falling, seems to understand
The lightest tug, and climbs back to our hand.

And when we've blown an essay or a test,
The book bag that imagined we were wise
Slumps on our bed, despondent and distressed;
The stuffed bear lifts us sadly shining eyes
And as it both reproaches and condoles,
Hints that all things have sympathies and souls.

Hence if somebody steals our bike, a chief
Concern is for *its* plight: We fear the thief
Will curse and kick it if it slips its chain,
Will score its rims when forced to change its tires,
Will smash its headlamp, leave it out in rain,
Till it, exhausted by abuse, expires.

Hence, too, our guilt—for few of us can flatter
Ourselves that we're good guardians of matter.
Despite materialistic appetites,
We let paint peel, tools rust, and don't take time
To give the car a bath till someone writes,
Wash Me, in the rear windshield's dust and grime.

It is, then, well that we retain a sense
That objects feel and suffer as we do:
It checks our carelessness and negligence.
It makes us see familiar things anew,
As when, condemned for having breached some rule,
I clapped chalk-choked erasers after school:

Pretending I made thunder helped me belt
Clouds from their tightly packed black strips of felt;
Returning to the classroom where all day
I'd fidgeted or bowed my head and prepped,
I set them in the blackboard's scalloped tray,
Cheered that they'd now breathe freely as they slept.

Didelphis Virginiana

The morning sun discovers an opossum
Run over at 18th and Robertson.
A mash of bloody organs, bone, and fur,
Distinguishable by its long bare tail,
It lies ironically in the crosswalk,
While traffic, two lanes each way, thunders past.
When the light turns, I hustle out, and scrape
And scoop it from the asphalt with a shovel;
In greedy expectation of the signal's
Changing again, cars gun their engines at me.

Many such creatures perish daily, nothing
In evolution having readied them
Against machinery: grief seems absurd.
Nature herself, ever pragmatic, is
Blithely indifferent to her child's departure.
Even as I inter it in the garden,
Dew-drenched calendulas and larkspur glisten;
A squirrel sniffs its way along a phone line,
Apparently examining for flaws
An argument the cable's carrying;
Having dropped anchor in the strawberries,
A mockingbird displays his wings, like someone
Opening the panels of an overcoat
To show he's come unarmed and should be trusted.

But our nocturnal forager is dead—
Native marsupial, nemesis of snails.

And if opossums have Elysium,
May this one's spirit be already there,
Shyly approaching and conversing with
Illustrious figures in its species' history;
May it, restored, probe with its pointed snout
Through a warm, everlasting night whose gardens
Are redolent with earth mold; may it turn,
In its fine paws, persimmons and blue plums
And munch them thoughtfully and peacefully,
The marvelous soft tissue of the brain
Safe in the skull.

                Meanwhile, I kneel and brush
Soil back into the grave, and, having tamped it,
Rise to resume my own diminished day.

Sepulveda Basin Mallards

They paddle through expanding
And overlapping wakes.
One glides in, cleared for landing,
And, with his breast for brakes,
Skids to a cushy halt,
Then makes a smooth turn shoreward.
Another, in the mood
To try a somersault
Or dabble for some food,
Pitches abruptly forward,

Tail straight up from the water.
Others appear to be
Content merely to potter
About in buoyancy.
Still others extract oil
From their rump glands to preen.
(Bills digging here and there,
Their lithe necks coil, uncoil,
As they check out, repair,
And keep their feathers clean.)

Just a mile off, two freeways
Cross like a scissors' shears;
The flyways and the seaways
Have narrowed with the years.
Still, in this watershed's

Low marshes, the ducks range
With cormorants and coots,
With grebes and buffleheads,
At home in old pursuits
And salutary change.

There, willow-overhung,
A mother leads the newer
Flotilla of her young,
Who, swivel-bonded to her
Mood (and direction) swings,
Veer neatly left and right.
On water-spanking feet,
A scaup sprints and flaps wings
And wills itself to meet
The requisites for flight.

Who wouldn't, though the day
Decline, be slow to leave
This place where egrets may
Remain on the qui vive,
Wading deliberately
Through chilly water plants?
Marsh wrens swoop after midges,
And the sharp eye can see
How fallen reeds are bridges
For hurrying-homeward ants

That cross a rivulet
Emptying in the pond.
Soon, darkness; but as yet

Birds call and, called, respond.
And mallards drift serenely
On the fresh inland tide—
Speculum feathers flashing,
Males lifting their heads greenly,
Some, as they're swimming, splashing
Their bills from side to side.

Yellow Birches

White birches enjoyed a poetic cachet
With which the poor yellows could never compete.
Their bark wasn't snowy, but ocher and gray
And wouldn't peel off, sheet by papery sheet;
Whenever I saw them, the thought that arose
Was, *Robert Frost's swinger didn't swing those.*

Yet they could perform some astonishing tricks.
Though shaded by hardwoods, they'd sprout up and reach
To the heights of the forest and loftily mix
In equable converse with maple and beech;
They frequently seeded, bizarre as it seems,
On the backs of great boulders in brooks and in streams.

They needed no more than some moisture and moss
To cover the rock with their tentacle roots;
Their grip once secure, they could shiver and toss
In the winds and encourage the health and pursuits
Of the birds and the deer that would visit and browse
On their bark and the catkins that hung in their boughs.

Except when wind freshened and set them astir,
They lacked the pure grace to attract or bewitch;
Yet any observer could see that they were
Adaptively canny in filling a niche
Where poets and juvenile males wouldn't tax
Their branches for morals and injure their backs.

White birches well merit their proper applause,
But I like the yellows and think that, on balance,
If forced to adopt an arboreal cause
I'd pick trees that alter their roots into talons
And whether in fields or on boulders in brooks
Can thrive without needing great soil or great looks.

Champlain Evening

The oars creak gently in their locks;
So tranquil is the lake
A ferry, several miles out, rocks
Her with its traveling wake.

It's easy work to which she bends:
When the oars dip, they craft
Small whirlpools she, with smooth strokes, sends
Spinning, like slow tops, aft.

Even when she arrests the oars
And turns ahead to view
(And imprint on her mind) the course
She wishes to pursue,

The boat coasts at a steady clip
Across the depths and shades,
While strings of under-droplets slip
From the suspended blades.

Snow

The soundless character
Of snow was like a mood.
Out after supper, we
Felt both thrilled and subdued:
Our street had been transfigured
Into a lovely waste
But for the cones of lamplight
Its boundaries effaced.

We'd play touch football, passes
Wobbling from mittened hands;
We'd skid round, lacking traction
That stopping or cutting demands.
We'd pause for barreling plows,
The night's true juggernauts,
That cast off fans of snow
Like ocean-slicing yachts.

Disbanding, we could hear
Long after we could see
Each other; night resumed
Its mute autonomy,
Emptied of us and filling
With the thick-slanting snows
Through which occasional cars
Would—tire chains jingling—nose.

Toward the Winter Solstice

Although the roof is just a story high,
It dizzies me a little to look down.
I lariat-twirl the cord of Christmas lights
And cast it to the weeping birch's crown;
A dowel into which I've screwed a hook
Enables me to reach, lift, drape, and twine
The cord among the boughs so that the bulbs
Will accent the tree's elegant design.

Friends, passing home from work or shopping, pause
And call up commendations or critiques.
I make adjustments. Though a potpourri
Of Muslims, Christians, Buddhists, Jews, and Sikhs,
We all are conscious of the time of year;
We all enjoy its colorful displays
And keep some festival that mitigates
The dwindling warmth and compass of the days.

Some say that L.A. doesn't suit the Yule,
But UPS vans now like magi make
Their present-laden rounds, while fallen leaves
Are gaily resurrected in their wake;
The desert lifts a full moon from the east
And issues a dry Santa Ana breeze,
And valets at chic restaurants will soon
Be tending flocks of cars and SUVs.

And as the neighborhoods sink into dusk
The fan palms scattered all across town stand
More calmly prominent, and this place seems
A vast oasis in the Holy Land.
This house might be a caravansary,
The tree a kind of cordial fountainhead
Of welcome, looped and decked with necklaces
And ceintures of green, yellow, blue, and red.

Some wonder if the star of Bethlehem
Occurred when Jupiter and Saturn crossed;
It's comforting to look up from this roof
And feel that, while all changes, nothing's lost,
To recollect that in antiquity
The winter solstice fell in Capricorn
And that, in the Orion Nebula,
From swirling gas, new stars are being born.

Gym Nights

Each giddy drop induced the trampoline
To launch me that much higher from its bed;
I feared I'd arc off to the side and land,
Like a defective rocket, on my head.
My brother would perform, as a routine,
A hundred sit-ups; then, with arms flung wide,
He'd fall back to the mat, as if he planned,
By way of encore, to be crucified.

Those Fridays, which the Y called "Family Nights,"
Drew a wide range of adepts to the gym.
A young man rocked above the pommel horse
Hands lifting as his legs swung under him;
A girl traversed, in leotard and tights,
The balance beam, despite slight teeterings;
Another rose, arms trembling, by main force
Into a midair handstand on the rings.

Amid it all, we were aware of sounds—
The twang that, when released, the high bar made,
Post-spring vibrations from a vaulting board,
And sneaker squeaks where basketball was played.
We'd join the basketball for shoot-arounds:
Sometimes a pair of shots in midflight met;
Sometimes they'd find the mark with one accord
And get hung up together in the net.

The kidding had an air of friendly doubt;
Nobody wished to touch a tender nerve.
Our folks' divorce, the trials of junior high,
Were treated with benevolent reserve.
If we occasionally curled about
And hauled up to the ceiling on a rope,
Was this escapist yearning? Even I
Knew not to get suspended on that trope.

Exertion let the fragile body glow:
The chest throbbed surely with its little sun.
In due course the custodian who controlled
The lights switched off their four banks, one by one.
We'd shower and we'd crunch home through the snow,
Lungs aching with the keenly frigid air.
I'd lift a hand to feel the way the cold
Created icicles in my damp hair.

Ethel Taylor

Bookkeeper for a small firm that made dyes,
She boarded at my grandparents' and loved
But had an allergy to strawberries.
Strawberry imagery adorned her note cards;
On her wall hung a still life of a dish
With strawberries, three apples, and a lemon;
Her teacups had a strawberry motif,
Red fruits and green stems twining round their bowls.
Such was her predilection and good nature
That she seized chances to help others savor
What fate and her physician had denied her;
And on snow-muffled evenings when I shoveled
My grandparents' front walk, she'd have me in
And serve me strawberry preserves on toast;
Or in the summer when I mowed the lawn
She'd hull fresh berries for me and present them
With shortcake and great dollops of whipped cream.

Having no relatives except a brother,
A railway mail clerk over in New Hampshire,
She shared her birthdays and her holidays
With our extended family and attended
With friends subscription-series plays, recitals,
And concerts at the university.
Whether from prelapsarian innocence
Or postlapsarian calculation, she
Had found and filled a niche that suited her;

And though that time was hard on single women,
She never seemed to rue her lot or wish
That she had had a family of her own.
She wasn't Robinson's Aunt Imogen,
Nor was I a young George, whose boyish charms
Could pierce a spinster with her childlessness.
However patiently she lent herself
To news of school or church-league basketball,
My volubility sometimes fatigued her;
And following one garrulous report,
She set her cup back coolly on its saucer
And said, "Aren't we a chatterbox today"—
Making a blush spring hotly to my cheeks
For having, in my vanity, imagined
That I'd been entertaining, when I'd merely
Been spraying words about, much in the way
That an untended hose, flopping and thrashing,
Jets water here and there at everyone
And everything in its vicinity.
The only sign that lack might haunt her life
Came when her company moved to Brattleboro:
She went with them, but, the next year, retired
Abruptly and returned to Burlington
And the familiar second-floor apartment
My grandparents kept set aside for her.
In retrospect, I realize how attached
She was to them and Burlington itself—
Its Church Street shops, its hillside situation
By Lake Champlain, and its broad views across
The water to the Adirondack Mountains.

Even four decades later, I can still
Picture her sitting room—the overstuffed
Armchair and sofa with lace doilies draped
Upon their arms and back; the ottoman,
Which proved the safest place for me to perch
Because remote from her framed, standing photos,
Her table lamps, and porcelain figurines;
The corner cupboard, which, designed to fit
The space where two walls met, enchanted me
With cleverly triangular shelves and drawers;
The Persian carpet upon which a sunbeam,
Dispersed in passing through a windowpane,
Might print a watery-prismed patch of rainbow;
The elm that overhung the roof and spattered,
After a rain, a second storm of drops
Down from its drenched and gust-swept foliage.
And thinking of these things, I feel a certain
Affectionate responsibility
Since, having been among the very youngest
Of her acquaintances, I may one day
Be the last person who remembers her.

In any case, whenever in the summer
I pick fresh strawberries and gently crush one
Against my palate with my tongue, and taste
The sunny warmth of the sweet pulp and juice,
I see her standing in her kitchenette
Some cricket-throbbing evening in July,
Neatly extracting, with a paring knife,
The calyxes from berries, or removing
The beaters from her mixer and suggesting

I lick the clinging whipped cream from their blades.
And of the duties that a lifetime gives us,
One of the happiest of mine has been
To listen as she chatted of her brother
Or of canoe-and-camping trips she took
When young—this woman I did not know well,
But for whom, for a time, I served as proxy
In the enjoyment of forbidden fruit.

Vermont Transit

Where Route 100 went climbing
    Northeast through wooded hills,
It passed the neighboring townships
    Of Eden and Eden Mills,
And the mere mile between them
    Enabled us to gauge
How quickly Paradise yielded
    To the Industrial Age.

Along the road were aspens
    With skittish, silvery leaves
And houses with upper windows
    Aligned to slanted eaves,
While sunny, wind-foraged meadows
    Cloud shadows scudded across
Suggested innocence darkened
    By knowledge and by loss.

It's true each village featured
    Things that belied its name:
Eden possessed a graveyard,
    While Eden Mills could claim
Lake Eden and some campgrounds.
    Yet, always, we'd recall,
Passing from one to the other,
    The old myth of the Fall.

Three decades and time zones west now,
    I'm sometimes pulled up short
Commuting on clogged freeways:
    I'll tune to a traffic report
Of closed ramps, fender benders,
    And fertilizer spills,
And I'll feel like I've left Eden
    And am heading for Eden Mills.

Henry and Elvis

When James deserts his novelistic muse
To write plays and seek popular acclaim,
When Presley jettisons his blue suede shoes
To act, their situations are the same:
They don't appreciate what makes them good.
You've energy and wit! we tell our heroes.
Why court the West End crowd or Hollywood?
Why crave Dean Martin's laurels or Pinero's?

They cannot hear, of course, and, for that matter,
Most hunger to be other than they are.
Prospects of universal genius flatter
The diva who would paint, the movie star
Become a bard, the physicist turned chef,
And athletes who imagine they can rap.
To do just one thing well is hard enough.
Drawn to the talent-knows-no-limit trap?

Recall the night *Guy Domville* was premiered
And how James, when the curtain fell, was led
To center stage, expecting to be cheered,
And was abused and hooted at instead.
Recall, too, *Double Trouble,* where the King,
Sashaying and exuding specious charm,
Performed clucks, oinks, and moos, obliged to sing
A "rocking" *Old MacDonald Had a Farm.*

A Muse

He's grateful for the thought-provoking rigors
She teaches, but he feels he is at best
A dunce who takes her topics and her figures
And renders them confusing or absurd:
Earnest, he is suspected of a jest;
Ironic, he is taken at his word.

When he grows histrionic with despair,
"Is this the man," she'll laugh, "who pledged me patience?"
She'll try to muss some sense into his hair
Or kiss a brow anxieties besiege.
And, charmed, he'll almost think her ministrations
Are born of love and not noblesse oblige.

At times she'll sit and sift through draft-filled folders
And tell him what to scrap or to pursue.
He'll stand behind her and massage her shoulders
Or lift and tuck behind her ear a tress,
Intuiting in the scent of her shampoo
Art's rich and magical suggestiveness.

At other times she's snappish or remote,
And nothing he can say seems worth her heeding.
In sunglasses, head scarf, and overcoat,
She'll blankly hurry past him on the street
Or spend whole rainy days absorbed in reading,
Legs curled beneath her in the windowseat.

No use, when this occurs, to cast a look
Of longing or cry out in recognition:
She'd only drop her eyes back to her book
Or leave him in her wake, bemused and checked.
Loneliness, too, is part of his tuition,
And faith is nothing if not circumspect.

The trick is not to hound her or ignore her,
But wait with an alert passivity.
She will again, if he just listens for her,
Approach with her old warmth and, by her arts,
Temper his voice with her voice so that he
Can speak the deeper language she imparts.

Faustina

Abandoning the garden she patrols,
She trots down the brick path from the garage,
And, flopping on the patio, curls and rolls
From side to side, inviting a massage.
We've quarreled over birds in recent days:
For beauty's and flight's sake, I take their part,
Whereas the interest that she displays
In avian life is strictly à la carte.

She stretches on her back; I scratch her chest.
My own back and left shoulder twinge and pinch
From when I jammed them diving to arrest
Her as she was absconding with a finch.
(Hindquarters seized, she whirled on me and hissed;
The bird shot free.) And now she cranes to draw
Notice to areas I've sometimes missed
Along her neck and underchin and jaw.

Should I exert myself on her behalf,
Whose instinct is to pillage and pursue?
She rises, wreathes her tail around my calf,
Then stands with her two hind paws on my shoe.
I've fed her, had her immunized and spayed,
But she defeats me in our clash of wills,
Darting off—little stray, rough renegade—
While I regret the laws that she fulfills.

Sad Epigrams

1. Hercules and the Poet

Jove's son slew Linus, who'd corrected
The youth's performance of a carol:
Thus all who judge the well-connected
And tin-eared do so at their peril.

2. Jerusalem Delivered

All night, crusading Tancred fought the foe,
Whom finally he killed and stripped of armor.
It was his Muslim mistress. Even so,
Men cannot recognize love till they harm her.

3. A Short History of Post-structuralism

Words don't match things, and authors are erased;
Reality reflects the theorist's taste.
Yet, to the grief of all, the text fights back,
Whether it's *Hamlet*, *Emma*, or Iraq.

At the Chautauqua Channel

Swelled by the recent storms, the channel rushes
Under the highway and across the beach,
Cutting a furious path to the Pacific.
The channel's banks, like calving glaciers, slide
Great slices of their sand into the torrent
Whose tumbling waters bear a wealth of refuse—
Styrofoam cups, beer cans, McDonald's wrappers,
Condoms, flip-flops, cigarette butts, and Pampers.
A short-billed mew gull stands on the far bank,
Watching the sorry spectacle flood past,
And, if she were a lexicographer,
"A wingless animal that litters" might
Well be her definition of a human.
Fronting the channel, the indignant sea
Deposits booming and mist-showering waves:
It fashioned life and sent it forth to land,
And this is how life's most commanding species
Returns the favor! High above the highway,
On the eroded palisades, a house
Hangs over the abyss—the exposed half
Of its foundation propped by giant stilts.
The mew gull, having seen enough, lifts off
And lets the stiff wind gust her toward the pier
Where weekday fishermen are casting lines
Out to the doubtful waters. Far to seaward,
More storm clouds gather, like the coming wrath
Of God or Nature or the God in Nature.

In a Eucalyptus Grove

Some small dark thing thrashed in the path;
And I, dumbfounded and afraid,
Recoiling from its agony,
Could not decipher, much less aid,

This lizard—was it?—or young snake.
Yet even as I stood aghast
A long thin leaf spun down upon
And quelled the shadow it had cast.

Black Phoebe

Her swoops are short and low and don't aspire
To more, it seems, than nature's common strife.
Perching, she strops her bill across a wire
As though she'd barbered in a former life.
When the wire rocks, she quickly dips her tail
A few times, and her balance doesn't fail.

If she displays an unassuming pride—
Compact, black-capped, black breast puffed to the sun—
The sentiment perhaps is justified:
Mosquitoes, gnats, and flies would overrun
Much of the planet within several years
But for her and her insectivorous peers.

Not prone, as are the jays, to talking trash,
She offers quieter companionship;
On summer days, when starlings flap and splash
And make the birdbath overspill and drip
Or empty out its basin altogether,
She seeks the shade and waits for cooler weather.

When autumn whips the plum tree to and fro
And rains slick its dark trunk, and pools collect
Among its exposed roots, and Mexico
Tempts most birds of the garden to defect,
It is a cheering check against chagrin
To think this is the place she'll winter in.

She makes, for now, a series of abrupt
Dives, lifts, and turns; from a tomato stake,
She spots a moth and darts to interrupt
Its course and then retrieves her perch to make
A thorough survey, though at no great height,
Of plants confided to her oversight.

The Middle Years

The subway station flashes from the dark;
Its name and its wall panel ads coast by.
She grips a handrail, poised to disembark,
As the car stops and settles with a sigh.
Doors slide open. She exits, and the stairs
Record the scuffing hurry of her feet;
The escalator past the turnstiles bears
Her steeply up a tunnel to the street.

The scene should look familiar, yet the sun
And the walk's harsh scintillae make her wince.
She senses that she could be anyone—
Not a museum's Curator of Prints
Who has a pair of cats and PhDs,
A widowed mother whom she calls each day,
And, for the past few weeks, anxieties
That she can neither pinpoint nor allay.

Work reassures her somewhat. She reviews
And signs off on the Annual Report;
The Office of Development has news
About a donor she would like to court;
A colleague's sent a basketful of fruit
(She helped launch an exhibit he designed),
Topped by a pomegranate, hurt en route,
Whose red seeds gleam within its fissured rind.

An omen, she reflects, may lie in this:
She's been divorced and lonely far too long
And is ripe for a metamorphosis
To a dark middle age with Mr. Wrong.
But, meanwhile, meetings claim her: the new wing
Has sucked up half the budget; paintings stowed
For years downstairs need deaccessioning;
The Board wants her to mount a show on Claude.

When she can finally get back to it,
Her office is all dark. The staff have gone.
She looks down from her window. Newly lit,
The streetlamps have soft gold coronas on;
The park looks eerie in autumnal mist.
Hearing doves flap and coo beneath the eaves,
She blesses sadly their romantic tryst.
The door falls locked behind her as she leaves.

She stops off at the florist's, then descends
Into the subway. Waiting for her train,
She shuts her eyes: stock's heavy, rich scent blends
With rustlings of the bouquet's cellophane.
Air rushes from the tunnel; people see
A light approaching. She prepares to board,
Though feeling like a grave Persephone
Reluctantly returning to her lord.

For Victoria, Traveling in Europe

By placing in its path an index card,
I catch an ant that scurries round the sink.
I take it (it came indoors with the chard)
And tilt it to the garden. May it link,
By bump-identifying, with a chum
Who'll guide it to its formicarium.

And may you, from your weeks abroad, return
To see these burgeoning tomato plants,
Whose heavy fruit appears to cause concern
Among supporting stakes now dragged askance.
And may you see these bean vines spiral to
The tepee summit of their rendezvous.

I, rootless in your absence, roll up sleeves
And, like a washerwoman, slosh and clean
Within the sink the chard's great crinkly leaves,
Lamenting that we cannot share cuisine,
But hoping, as with plants from seeds we sowed,
We'll soon resume a rhizogenic mode.

Swimming in Winter

Palo Alto, 1977

On cold, wet days, I didn't use the gym
But patronized the outdoor pool instead:
I worried that if no one came to swim
It might feel lonely and dispirited.

It clearly couldn't thank me for my care;
One time, though, its Olympic-size expanse
Gusted inviting ripples to me where
I shed my Windbreaker and training pants.

I liked to think of that when, in the rain,
I'd dive and surface to an easy crawl
And do my lunch laps, staying in my lane,
Swimming away the winter's cold, dark miles
Between the turning wall and finish wall,
Tracking the bottom line's small square blue tiles.

August

In recent weeks, the level of the lake
Has fallen, and the reef declares itself,
Although the larger waves still, when they break,
Submerge with whooshing suds its broad shale shelf.
Here trembling fragments of the sky appear
On pools in hollows as the waters clear.
Here gulls resettle draining rocks, while out
Where the wind's brushstroke makes a cloud a plume,
A man who guides his sailboat's swift career
Leans hard upon the tiller, comes about,
And ducks the cross-deck swinging of the boom.

A boy an early swim has fortified
Discovers it's still hot work to parade
Bright lawns or turn his mower on its side
To knock free dew-soaked grass that clogs the blade.
Using the apron of his undershirt,
He sponges off his brow to stay alert,
And actually looks forward to his shift
At the garage where, if obliged to toil,
He'll mostly just draw, check, and reinsert
Dipsticks or, under a hydraulic lift,
Drain oil pans of their engine-weary oil.

Meanwhile, the garden's thriving: rows once strict
Are now a rioting of salad greens;
Zucchinis threaten that, if left unpicked,
They'll burgeon to the size of submarines;

Muskmelons, with their warm, rough, webby skin,
Delight the touch of those who bring them in.
Shelled peas go rattling into pots and bowls;
String beans need gathering every several hours;
And as a measure of how hot it's been,
The broccoli's slipped its vegetable controls
And bolted into spiky yellow flowers.

In such rich warmth, it's easy to relax
And hard to credit calendars and clocks,
Which register, among their other facts,
The shorter days, the coming equinox.
When forced indoors toward evening by a storm,
Children drape quilts on tipped-down chairs to form
Tunnels and tents from which adults are barred;
And when the thunder and hard showers wane,
And, in the dripping dusk, gnats drift and swarm,
A woman home from work walks through her yard
And dumps a canvas hammock of its rain.

Nor does it seem that summer soon will pass
When darkness falls and switches on the crickets.
A croquet ball, though stalled now in the grass,
Dreams of tomorrow's journey through the wickets;
Breeze wakes a porch's wind chimes, and promotes
Their pleasantly confused and liquid notes;
A full moon rises, orange and immense,
Though climbing causes it to shrink and bleach;
A streamer on a flagstaff snaps and floats
Above the cove; in dark rooms, sleepers sense,
All night, waves crashing on the rocks and beach.

The Sweet Peas

The season for sweet peas had long since passed,
And the white wall was bare where they'd been massed;
Yet when that night our neighbor phoned to say
That she had watched them from her bed that day,
I didn't contradict her: it was plain
She struggled with the tumor in her brain
And, though confused and dying, wished to own
How much she'd liked the flowers I had grown;
And when she said, in bidding me good night,
She thought their colors now were at their height—
Indeed, they never had looked lovelier—
The only kind response was to concur.

Thereafter, as a kind of rite or rule,
Each autumn when the days turned damp and cool,
I'd sow peas gathered from the last year's pods.
I'd watch as young plants, bucking storms and odds,
Mounted the net and buds appeared on stems
While, using self-supporting stratagems,
Fine tendrils twined in midair, each to each,
Or to the mesh of screens within their reach
Until the vines and blossoms waved aloof
Of net and eaves in full view of the roof,
As if reporting, situated so,
News of the heavens to the yard below.

And I'd recall her, who had loved their scent,
But who, in spite of my encouragement,
Was shy of picking them until I said
They flowered more copiously if harvested.
(Red blooms came earliest, and, when they'd peaked,
The purples followed, and the salmon-streaked;
All equally attracted moth and bee.)
Meanwhile, her phone call gathered irony:
If, at the end, she'd summoned back somehow
Those vanished sweet peas, their descendants now
Returned the favor, having been imbued
With her departed grace and gratitude.

When blossoms—each with banner, wings, and keel—
Stir in the warmth above me while I kneel
And weed around the bottom of the plants,
I sometimes think that, if they had the chance,
They'd sail off after passing bird or cloud.
I sometimes hope that, if it was allowed,
She felt within her what she loved when she
Passed from this to that other mystery
And kept, by way of comfort, as she went,
The urge to complication and ascent
Which prints such fresh, bright signatures on air
That they are read when they're no longer there.

The Faithful Widower

The cat loves breakfast, so the man won't stint:
He fills her dish. The field is smooth with snow,
Which, in dawn's twilight, has a bluish tint.
The eastern sky, profoundly indigo,

Holds Mars and Venus. *Let them be,* he thinks.
He's had his run at passion and at glory;
The trophies of the bully and the minx
Mean less now than this kitchen's inventory—

Dark coffee dripping into its carafe,
A cat crouched to the meal her human caters,
A white plate with an English muffin half,
Gold butter melting in its toasted craters.

Starr Farm Beach

Although the beach, with its adjacent *r*'s,
Alluded to a dairy farm nearby,
We liked to think that, on the shoreline, stars
Were sown and grown and gathered for the sky.
Along the cliffs that led there, we would try
To find good foot- and handholds, and would weigh
The merits of the low road and the high
Or scan the waters north towards Malletts Bay.

Some evenings, from the cliff face, we'd review
The early piercing stars above the lake
And disregard their long-ago debut
To guess which were of recent, local make.
And we imagined if we stayed awake
All through the night, we'd see ghost gleaners, bent
Over the shallows, choosing stars to take
At dawn back with them to the firmament.

We loved swifts that performed wild swoops and swings
Over the lake in unobstructed air;
We loved fish that, in sudden surfacings,
Nabbed supper with quick piscine savoir-faire.
But we best loved stars rising here and there,
Whether from hopes of something we might sow
Or from a lonely impulse to declare
The kinship of the lofty and the low.

Printed by Printforce, United Kingdom